# SOUNDINGS

*Georgia A. Greeley*

LAUREL
POETRY
COLLECTIVE

*For my family,
friends,
mentors,
all those who have filled my life
with love, knowledge, and hope.*

### Acknowledgments

Poems in this collection which first appeared in other publications, in current or earlier versions, include: "Grandma Johnstone's Closet" in *Soup From Stones* (April 1982), "Lift versus Drag" in *Sidewalks* (Volume #9, 1995); "Equal Sign" in *Dust & Fire* (Annual Anthology of Women's Writing, Bemidji State University, 1995); "Of the Body" in *A New Name for the Sun* (Laurel Poetry Collective, 2003); "The Last Word" in *Pulling for Good News* (Laurel Poetry Collective, 2004); "Motorcycle: Then & Now" in *Ignited* (Laurel Poetry Collective, 2006).

Quotation on page 57 is from Phillis Levin, "Part," http://www.poemhunter.com/p/m/poem.asp?poem=187452 (accessed 1/20/2006).

Particular thanks go to all the members of Laurel Poetry Collective; my small group; my laughter-filled letterpress team; Sylvia Ruud, who designed this book; and Nancy Walden and Deborah Keenan, who read and responded to this manuscript. Long-term thanks go to all my friends and fellow writers in the Lake Street Writers Group.

© 2006 by Georgia A. Greeley

All rights reserved.

ISBN 0-9761153-9-5

Printed in the United States of America.

Published by Laurel Poetry Collective
1168 Laurel Avenue, St. Paul MN 55104
www.laurelpoetry.com

Book design by Sylvia Ruud

Library of Congress Cataloging-in-Publication Data
Greeley, Georgia A.
    Soundings / Georgia A. Greeley.
        p. cm.
    ISBN 0-9761153-9-5 (alk. paper)
    I. Laurel Poetry Collective. II. Title.
PS3607.R4295S67 2006
811'.6—dc22
                                    2006000977

CONTENTS

prologue: River                                    6

part one: Gardens

Mother                                             8
Third Daughter                                     9
Bugs & Blossoms                                   10
Red                                               11
Sugar Peas                                        12
Okra                                              13
Breathing Color                                   14
Why Flowers?                                      15
Litany                                            16

part two: Artists

Almost Paul Cézanne                               18
Elevation – Above Tree Line                       19
Pause                                             20
Still Life with Fruit                             21
Hush, I'm Coming...                               22
Letter to Picasso                                 23

## part three: Vehicles

| | |
|---|---|
| Lift versus Drag | 26 |
| Motorcycle: Then & Now | 27 |
| Unmarked Crossing | 28 |
| Flight Time | 29 |
| Driving the Alaska Highway | 30 |
| Down Randolph Hill | 32 |

## part four: Family

| | |
|---|---|
| Father | 34 |
| Cabin Conversation | 35 |
| Night Reading | 36 |
| Covenant Renewed | 37 |
| My Son's Colors | 38 |
| Equal Sign | 39 |
| Paddy | 40 |
| Mother's Hands | 41 |
| Grandma Johnstone's Closet | 42 |
| Amy | 44 |
| Jim | 45 |

## part five: Poetry & Process

| | |
|---|---|
| Square Labor | 48 |
| Subtle Shifts | 49 |
| Of the Body | 50 |

| | |
|---|---|
| Between | 51 |
| Don't Open the Door, Dark Will Leak Out! | 52 |
| Choking | 55 |
| Rooted in White Space | 56 |
| Out of Context | 57 |

## part six: Cancer

| | |
|---|---|
| Parts | 60 |
| What Size? | 62 |
| Reconstruction? | 63 |
| What is the word I'm looking for? | 64 |
| Mirror Image | 65 |
| Prostheses | 66 |
| Containers | 67 |
| Silhouette | 68 |

## part seven: People, Ghosts & Angels

| | |
|---|---|
| She Who Must Be Obeyed | 70 |
| Honky Tonk Angels | 72 |
| Immaculate Conception | 73 |
| Ronnie | 74 |
| Living Bones | 75 |
| The Last Word | 76 |
| Lost & Found | 77 |

## epilogue: Breathing 79

# River

This river, named after a crow's wing,

makes me feel light.

Just sitting on the dock above,

or watching it move past the window from inside my cabin,

without even one finger tracing a tiny wake upon its surface,

these waters wash through me,

soak and ease the anxious cord around my heart,

repattern each thrum-hum pulse to match the current's

elemental rhythms and flow;

somehow this river stretches my heart,

until it can hold

all it is given to hold.

part one:
# Gardens

## Mother

Leaning over delicate blue blossoms
my mother created hybrid bachelor buttons
as the sun beat down on her shoulders
and her sweat seeped into the soil,
salting the earth.
She was tied to her world by five young
children, the first three birthed before she was 21.
One nosy neighbor was puzzled
as to why she took the time to try to make a bluer blue
in a petal certainly brought to completion by God.
Undaunted, she would gently shake the pollen
from a stamen of the bluest male flower
and dust the pistil of the bluest female—
dropping yellow stars into a tiny petaled universe
to create a blue
that would make the sky shiver.

## Third Daughter

I don't want the flowers.
I want the words
to work as petals
pistils and stamen
the meaning
to be the haunting fragrance,
an aftertaste of words
in the reader's mind.

## Bugs & Blossoms

My second hibiscus consorts daily
with white flies
that suck at her leaves
and ravish her flowers.
She preens by the window,
popping buds in the northern light
while I water, trim, pinch, and pluck,
mothering this mother
that daily births delicate
coral blossoms.

My first hibiscus
died from one of my
well-intentioned treatments
to rid her lemon-yellow blooms
of those pesky white flies.
Plants or people,
when and how to act
is the crabby, constant question.

All my children are grown now,
yet I still sit, struggling with my hibiscus,
trying to get it right.
I'm never sure how to cherish the plant
succor the roots
give each finely veined blossom what it needs,
so petal by tightly wrapped petal
the flower will open, vulnerable,
awakened, and ready.

# RED

*On being envious of a color-blind husband*

I am uncomfortable with color
even when it's called hue.
Perhaps that's why I garden;
you see, my garden is somehow out of control.
No matter how I plan, the bright red cannas
come up coral, the kaleidoscopic
color scheme turns out yellow;
and the blue garden I order
comes full of replacements.

Blue, a color symbolizing Heaven in Eastern icons,
comes in so many colors.
They were out of the blue I wanted so I got all these
other blue things instead to grow next to my almost blue
but really purple clematis...
And somehow I still ended up monochromatic, except
for some alpine rosy bells that popped up right in the middle
of the blues and whites; I could have pretended they were
weeds and pulled them up, yet it seemed so odd to be afraid of pink—
I mean *pink*—can you imagine an artist afraid of color?

And the whole plant doesn't come up one color,
so there is always all sorts of green to deal with,
and my garden continues
quite out of control.

Do you suppose it was a red or green
apple that Eve allegedly offered Adam in that
other garden? I think he would have balked
at red—
brilliant, shiny, sensual red,
held gently in the palm of Eve's hand—
Red!

# Sugar Peas

*for Jonis & our gardens*

Perhaps you're right, for you,
for me,
it's time to quit gardening;
all this rooting and uprooting
takes time,
pulls at us like a child's needs,
emotional energy displaced,
spread under dirt,
forced down around dry hard seeds we
rush to moisten, loosen,
nurture...

But there is that thrill of watching a supple
green shoot
push its way through darkness
to stand delicately fresh,
exposed...

It's hard to break
this habit of caring for
dried out seeds and vulnerable seedlings uncurled
like babies fresh out of sleep;
so I took your suggestion
and planted the sugar peas.

Maybe next year
I'll let the soil lie fallow,
let it burst forth in its own
inevitable crop of weeds.

Yet how can I
deny
this insistent urge to plant?

## Okra

A feminine flower
sturdy as a weed yet
hidden
by grape-shaped leaves shivering
in the hot summer wind.

One wind gust reveals
five yellow petals surrounding
a deep purple center
dusted softly
with fertile powder.

Curled undersides
veined in dark red
cling
to an ascending fruit,
green,
covered with tiny soft hairs.

Tubular, rigid,
light green vertical lines move
the eyes and fingers
to the uncut
curved tip.

Heated,
okra takes on a deeper hue,
holds its shape,
and releases a clear
slippery fluid.

## Breathing Color

Lush.
No other word
is ripe enough for
this end-of-summer abundance:
green leaves, green grass, green
growth until one can
breathe green like air.

Grapevines think
the night coolness is Spring
and throw out new shoots
with budding blossoms.

Tomatoes tilt toward
red and weigh in the hand like
a woman's breasts,
engorged and heavy.

Lush.
This lingering burst of green struts a bit
before the slanting breeze of autumn screams
a kaleidoscope of color—
one last wild wail to greet
the wide and wintry white.

## Why Flowers?

They have petals soft and twitchy as cats' ears
stand in the rain with no clothes on
root in air, water, or soil
sing at our wakes
scent our graves
stun our senses with vibrant color—

pull us fully into the moment.

# Litany

My country chooses war;
children are killed;
men die, women are raped;

I choose to draw beautiful images.


People are without homes,
without clothes, without warmth,
many don't have enough to eat;

I use my hands to make beautiful books.


Men and women still haven't
learned to love one another or live together;
families struggle and fall apart;

I use my eyes, ears, and heart to write poetry.


I sit in the middle of my garden, pulling weeds,
sweating, smelling the mix of fragrance, earth and body,
and I can't let myself stop;

some of us, all of us, have to insist on beauty and hope.

part two:
Artists

## Almost Paul Cézanne

So many colors;
glasses and plates talk to each other,
clink endless secrets.
I listen hard but can't hear,
only see,
hardy hues warming each other.

There is a culminating point,
or a soul,
always—out of view,
fleeing the spot closest to the eye.

That is enough.

## Elevation – Above Tree Line

She reads the words
about artists
and looks and looks into
each painted image.

Colors and words layer
one upon the other
like snow building quietly
on a mountain's edge.

Pausing in the stillness,
the crack and thunder of avalanche
leaves her
breathless and shaking.

## Pause

The painter selects colored pigments.
Bristles kiss canvas.
Paint is pushed by the brush.
The canvas holds wet, mindful strokes, glistening images,
and life continues moving and breathing
around the painter.

But the moment painted stands still—

for people,
strangers,
to come,
stand still,
and look.

To see what is missed in the living.

## Still Life with Fruit

The orange is split.
The banana rots.
The peach peeks darkly
out of a frayed cloth wrapping,
and one, single, solitary
quarter-sized piece of orange peel
dries alone,
edges curled and harsh
to the touch.

Eat quickly—
before all goodness
vanishes.

## Hush, I'm Coming...

I can't help it that empty boxes and
other leftover things
call my name
(a curved length of metal)
so I pick them up
(part of a muffler in the street)
and bring them home;
I know they all belong somewhere,
(a sheet of wire mesh covered in orange plastic)
in a collage, a sculpture, in
Joseph Cornell's coffin, but
I don't have the time right now so
they wait in two overflowing boxes on the very top shelf
of my closet, dribbling onto the workspace
in my studio, interrupting me with
delicate, unassuming coughs,
as if to say they are tired of hovering
in stillness
in the dark
waiting for my touch.

## Letter to Picasso

When I saw so much of your
work together, images piled
on top of each other in my brain,
a great, clattering noise of color,
but it was your eyes—
from the personal photos interspersed throughout the show—
that stayed with me.
Those dark eyes and their
confrontational glare,
a glare which took up residence in
many of the paintings, peered out,
particularly from contorted female bodies,
eyes saying,

"Look.　See.　Cry.　Laugh."

It wasn't until halfway through the show,
when I began smiling in response
to that demanding twinkle in your eyes,
that I could get past the surface of your paintings,
feel the energy of each stroke,
the guffaw of paint splashed on canvas,
the passion beneath the peculiar.

I walked out laughing.

part three:
Vehicles

# Lift versus Drag

There is a moment
when the plane rushes forward
that you feel a pause within the rush
and know the air is holding you
the metal
the machine
all the people sitting next to you
breathing in that unseeable substance
which is supporting you above the ground
pushing you forward.
And you learn in that slight sigh
of machine upon the air
that you trust what cannot be seen.
And you see that each day you participate
in a thousand unthought
miracles
as simple as taking a breath
as complex as hurtling through the sky.

And you sit within the knowing
watch the top side of heaving clouds
accept the foil-wrapped peanuts and iced pop
as the smallest part of the offering.

And later
there is that spot in time
when the wheels first touch the runway
the air gives up its burden but not its speed
and brakes are applied
and applied, and applied,
and you learn with every cell of your body
how good it is to stop.

# Motorcycle: Then & Now

Permit in pocket, at age 19,
I slung my leg over the seat of our 650 Triumph
and settled in for my first solo drive.

When I got out of the city, started
flowing up and down those backcountry roads,
time shifted into reverse; I was again an
11-year-old girl unknowingly
riding a stallion into a field
of mares in heat. The warm body
between my legs was out of control;
I reveled in the strong wind
tugging at my hair, the thunderous
rhythm of hooves beating the earth, and
muscles rippling like a heavenly undertow beneath me.
I was hooked.

But after only six months,
lots of non-motorcycle life intervened;
our bike was sold.

At 42, despite making my husband nervous,
I bought a 1982 Honda MB5,
got a tattoo, earned my motorcycle endorsement,
and started riding again. It wasn't the same.

But it was enough.

# Unmarked Crossing

It doesn't start as a noise
but a vibration
and even when it's not night
it feels like it's coming at you out of the dark
this rhythm that chugs through your body
before your ears hear the sound
before your eyes see the cars flashing through the spaces
between the trees across the river.

If it's daylight and you're busy
what you first hear sounds
like a sudden gust of air moving through the leaves
but what catches you, pulls you to alertness
is that it doesn't stop
or slow
but gets louder until you hear the rhythm
feel the ground rumble
an alien heartbeat rising through your feet.

If you're asleep
you are awakened by a loud pulse
shaking the bed
just in time for a howl that pierces the darkness
naming this unmarked crossing at speeds
in excess of 50 miles per hour—
and your mind mouths the word "train."

No matter when or where
night-day-standing-sitting
that noise
pushing through trees like air expanding lungs never before filled
becomes a train
slicing by on rails hooked to the crust of the earth
and every time its whistle blows—
something     cracks     open

## Flight Time

To be lifted by air
and soar miles above the earth
is one definition of beauty unrestrained.

I look out my small window,
and the arching line of wing
appears to be the edge of the earth,
holding the sunset above it for hours.

I look below me and see
matte-white, snow-swept land,
looking like a giant motherboard,
a vulnerable path of connections
unseen, except from this heightened point of view.

In this bullet-shaped room stuffed with strangers,
the earth slowly darkens below me.
Each time I see a light,
akin to the age-old signal fire,
I send back an answer—

>   I see
>   I follow
>   I will arrive

# Driving the Alaska Highway

Flimsy metal walls protect you from wind,
rain, rocks, bugs—otherness. The world can
shrink fully into the perimeter of one 4x4 truck.

My husband built a platform to rest over the
wheel wells of our 8-foot truck bed. A futon
fit on top of the platform with room to spare.
I made special boxes, which slid under
our makeshift bed, and we carefully planned
what gear, supplies, or clothes belonged
in each box. I attached a hook on one end
of a broom handle to pull out the boxes pushed
past arm's reach.

It felt brave and dangerous to pull the edges
of our lives into this small space and drive
3,000 miles northwest. I felt a daughter
to pioneer women, even though my oases
were gas stations, campgrounds, and grocery
stores, not streambeds or hunting grounds.

We sped along on four thick rubber tires, yet
I felt deeply our modern loss, the
daily connection earlier peoples experienced
through constant contact with, and dependence
upon, the earth.

I looked out at the changing colors of landscape,
rolled down my window, smelled clover
fields, dust, wild grasses, and blossoming weeds.

After two days it was easy to imagine this
was all there was—me, Jim, and the road—except for
the pesky traffic, and those cities, which popped up
at intervals both frequent and spare. I found I didn't
want to write; I just wanted to look, breathe,
and look some more.

We drove through valleys, plains, mountains, tundra,
country that looked like picture postcards framed
by the metal oblongs of windshield and side windows.
We waited for goats and caribou to cross our roadways.

After seven weeks and 6,000 miles, I was ready to leave the truck;
but not what it had taught me. Sometimes you have to leave
what you know. Sometimes, it's good to measure your
life by what you can fit into one full-sized truck.

## Down Randolph Hill

The bus motion is bumpy
pushes at my body
as if it were a plane
taxiing down the runway
unsure if it's actually going to fly.

Pushed into the seat
pushed out of the seat
by momentum out of my control—

> like Roman dying of a brain tumor,
> Kate & Bill walking towards the river in Luxor as terrorists kill 64,
> Janet & baby surviving a three-day breech labor...

Birth and death punctuate each moment
whether I sit on the bus
or in my studio
cutting paper and spreading glue,
ignoring the certainty
I will soon be doing very different work
to earn a living.

Today
tilted steeply downhill
bounced into and out of well-worn seats
I am thrown into skittish dreams of flight
with the unshakable belief—

liftoff is possible.

part four:
Family

# Father

My father once told me
his favorite colors were
black and yellow.
This night, the stars winked
yellow in the night sky
as he stood thigh-deep in the
lake retrieving my tangled
fishing line from an overhanging tree.

The way he named those colors,
the child I was wondered if he wanted
to wrap himself in those heaven-bound
hues and pretend
to be someone else,
somewhere else.

Another time he told me
he was a grin-and-bear-it-tone.
But once I heard him sing
in a deep voice
rich with colors
which harmonized with the evening stars.
Just once.

## Cabin Conversation

Flashes. Night stars.
Needlepoints of pulsing light.
Mom and I sit quietly on the porch.
Underneath the floorboards
chipmunks claw cool dirt for seeds.
My feet beat counterpoint,
toenails itching to mimic the humble deed.
She thumbs Bible pages;
silently, I rhyme hum & thrum & thumb.
She reads and whistles through her teeth, then speaks—

"I trust you respected yourself too much
              to have sex before you got married?"

The eaves release a wicked squeak.
I stand and floorboards creak;
holding my breath, I look up to the stars.

Blinking images:
        three non-virgin births
        seven years sharing a marriage bed
        my childhood nightmares slowly unsewn
        three thriving children, almost half-grown
I sigh and silently decide:

*That's my business. Mine alone.*

Yes, the blinking stars agree.
I bend over and kiss the top of her head.
"I'm going to bed."

I leave her—
one thumb stuck in the Bible reliving old memories—
trying to unmake a sin
everyone else has forgiven.

## Night Reading

There is so much about our
marriage that follows no common logic.

My husband, among the many other richly
complex things he is and can be, is color-blind and dyslexic.
For some reason, he chose to marry me,
an artist and a writer.

Over the years, one of our biggest recurring
arguments was over the time
I spent reading. The underneath
argument, the real one, was that words
took me away. From him. From
our children. He became moody
when I would read on *family*
vacations; when I chose to vacation elsewhere,
so to speak.

Reading took time he didn't feel he had to spend,
so whenever he could get away with it,
Jim chose not to read anything but newspapers
or work-related materials, until after he retired.
I waited 28 years to lie beside him at night,
reading books in companionable silence.

But that's not all. A newfound grace,
uncommon logic, has been formed by
the reading time and topics he now chooses.
He reads about and makes from scratch all the bread we eat;
he makes beautiful stained-glass windows, letting me pick the colors;
he restores old furniture and gives it new life.
Sometimes, I even get irritated
when he won't turn out the light at night
because *he's* still reading.

## Covenant Renewed

We half smile
fidget on the worn deck behind the house
mother and son
and each wonder how
to say good bye—this time.

It's not like the first time he left
and may not even be the last, nor is it
one of many unmarked partings between
his childhood fears and adult silences.

But I look into his eyes now
and try to guess
what person, newly faceted
will appear before me like some strange man
who says he's my son
who calls out—

"Mom, I'm home"

should he ever choose
to name it 'home' again.

## My Son's Colors

The long, silent view of his closet
is of earth tones—brown, green, khaki, and maroon.
His work shirts hang like a subdued,
horizontal rainbow.

He was a child of such brightness,
his emotions spilling out in primary colors
yellow—red—blue
outrageously happy,
supremely sad, seldom in between;
but always amazingly awed
by the world and what he found in it.

I flew thousands of miles to
visit him, an adult living alone in Alaska.
I walk quietly through his apartment and
my eyes soak up the visible artifacts of his life,
seeking the bright and tender energy
of the child I remember.

I find a red-checkered wool shirt,
yellow tee, royal blue down vest,
sense the hidden energy it takes to live so far from home
in a world of glaciers, mountain peaks, ocean tides,
near the surge of spawning salmon,
bright red,
pushing against all odds,
against the cold, constant current.

## Equal Sign

My algebra teacher once said,
"Never do something to one side of the equation,
unless you also do it to the other."
But how do I weigh the touch of
my suckling infant's hand
gently stroking my breast against
an unwritten poem?

This same male mentor of facts said,
"Once you learn how to add, subtract,
divide and multiply, I'll understand how
you get the answers right."

Add three children and
subtract 100 nights of sleep—
divide the husband by 2 and
carry the remainder on your back—
add three unwritten poems, one scribbled short story and
multiply the cost of one pound of hamburger
by the number of drawings that cloud your dreams
making your fingers twitch in the dark—
then balance this equation by the time
it takes to drain the dishwater out of the sink—
all the while trying to finger a rhyme into the scuzzy
ring left on the porcelain.

Balancing this equation hurts.

I aced algebra,
and I truly did learn how to add, subtract, divide and
multiply,
but right now—
I just can't figure out where
to put the equal sign.

# Paddy

I watched men step onto
the moon as I sat weighted
to the floor of my apartment
by the round mound of
child growing within me. My
heart touched the gravelled
craters as my daughter swam
in the amniotic waters our
bodies shared. This girl child,
once born, never wanted to
stay placed. This moon child
born to flit among the stars
was ready to leave home at
only four years of age—
confident her earth, her family,
would always stay in the sun's
orbit so she could occasionally
warm herself in its presence.
Those astronauts who took
one small step for mankind
snuck into my daughter's dreams
and stole her away as surely as
if they had swiped her from my womb.

## Mother's Hands

It was dark in the church
with so much space above me—
thick, full air,
and mother's hands,
with short, clean, rounded fingernails
and veins that carved
their way into the surface of
her skin.

I always wanted to take one of my fingers,
just one,
and press with my fingertip,
press until the protruding vein
closed;
one vein wall flat against the other
closed—blood stopped.

Even the thought felt
powerful: to stop my mother's blood.
I would kneel there,
afraid in that huge hovering space,
as Latin chants
rolled over and shivered through me,
hands flat, pressed tightly together in a
perfect imitation of prayer.

Years later, as I sit in church remembering,
my eldest daughter
slides her five-year-old hand into mine
and without thinking I stroke the soft, unmarked skin,
look down and see—
my hand in my mother's hand,
the fingertip
searching out the enlarged
pulsing vein.

# Grandma Johnstone's Closet

How dark
that closet was,
shadows of clothes moving
as I passed to
a hidden
dresser drawer of games.
The clothes barely
touched
the top of my head.
I was so small,
or were you so tall,
your hands
just above eye level,
long legs rising
out of feet
kept in sturdy black shoes.
If my eyes walked up
the large mountain of you,
your head seemed
always so far away,
blocking the ceiling light,
strands of hair
straying from the long
gray braid
that always encircled
your head.
No face—
I can't remember your face,
but I almost hear
your voice,
a low, constant tone
enveloping me in warmth
like the large
green silk quilt
which held me secure in your bed
in a house
that wasn't mine—

except for one closet
shadowed and
filled with secrets
just for me.
But one day
dad came home early
and said you were
dead.

He moved strangely
as if his arms
and legs were not
quite connected to his body;
and his face, so pale,
held no tears to wash away
his mother's death.

It felt like
rain that day.
Mom and dad whispered in dark
cloudy corners
to keep me from hearing
but I heard.

You shot yourself
in the head
and weren't found till morning.
It wasn't
until I asked for
my treasures from
the secret closet drawer
and watched
mom and dad's faces press
into whiteness
that I knew
you did it
in my closet.

No one told me
but once
I heard Aunt Peg
say quietly to dad
none of the toys
could be saved;
there was too much blood.

                                                Mom got your china.
                                           Dad got grampa's guns.
                                    Aunt Peg got your brooch.
                                                      Everyone
                                          got a piece of you
                                                        but me.

# Amy

She is the third child of parents
who were both third children.
Amy says being youngest and third makes a difference,
like the contrast of sun and moon,
one is cold dark light,
the other all bright white heat.
She teases us, sometimes dark light,
sometimes white heat, sometimes both.

After Peace Corps training,
she was sent deep into Paraguay
to teach farmers farming—
but too many men wore guns tucked into their pants
and were friendly in the wrong way.

Alone in the stifling jungle heat,
she chose safety,
walked away from her work site,
took her freckled fair skin
and slender body
back home—
and felt good about it.

This child who at 14 couldn't stay
overnight at a friend's home without getting a
stomachache, now relishes setting herself
down in a strange country, climate, and culture,
learning how to make this unknown place her own.

Experience. Understanding. Acceptance.
One. Two. Three.
My Amy is a female trinity who gathers all those willing
into her sphere
and shows them how to follow strange, difficult trails safely.
This third child of third children works daily for peace,
       dark light, bright white heat,
              she carefully marks our way…

# JIM

I've often wondered how
the world looks to my husband:
color-blind, the grass is not green.
How the world sounds to him:
dyslexic, words do not always open.
One of the first things I knew about him
was that he owned a telescope.
For looking.
For gazing at the stars.
As a young couple on a hill in the country,
backs to the ground,
we lay in the grass at a time when
the day had turned to black and white,
stars and night.
He reached for my hand and said,
"We are in the middle of the heavens.
We can fly without moving a muscle.
We are flying, right now."
Black and white,
darkness and light,
a journey through the heavens holding hands.

What more could we possibly need?

part five:
Poetry & Process

## Square Labor

I have this urge
to give birth to a clean sheet
of paper, freshly typed,
no errors,
something I can control;
a thing that doesn't drool,
mess diapers,
and only occasionally awakens me
from a sound sleep.

## Subtle Shifts

*for Ethna and her poem zone*

Light shines more clearly
though nothing physical has changed.

The water's ripple
takes on a sharper edge
slicing air into chunks of squared breath.

Birdsong triggers the forgotten
meter of a nursery rhyme, sharp
chirping music
cracks through memory and time—door
to an altered universe where

The aroma lifting from one tiny
lily of the valley
offers up the ghosts of our grandmothers,

And piles words upon the tongue
from an opened heart.

## Of the Body

There is a knowledge
inside the body
similar to a thin skin, unseen,
between the epidermis and the muscle layer.

Sometimes it simply perfuses
like blood, which feeds each cell oxygen,
and resides quietly
like a breath taken in deep sleep
and other times
it bristles the hair on one part of your neck.

There is a way you know
that something is poetry,
or real,
by the way it
makes bones itch
tongues lie flaccid
people you love
suddenly
appear as strangers
before heart or mind has time to react.

A knowing
more quick and keen
than death.

## Between

The places between the puzzle pieces
count.
Cause the connections to happen.
Paper-thin,
squared or multi-lobed,
the space not being filled
causes
sight,
forms the shapes & colors—

holes full of all that isn't there.


Like a curious rabbit
you jump into the hole,
see objects upside down,
touch, taste, and smell sideways,
try to be comfortable falling—

until you exit the other side.


Startled,
you begin looking
for another maze-like opening,
wiggle your whiskers,
bare your teeth—

and step over the edge.

*"The presence or absence of light—the lighted
surface or the shadowed surface—delineates form, substance."*
—3-D Design Text, 1980

## Don't Open the Door, Dark Will Leak Out!

But don't you want to open it,
just a peek, to see what *kind* of dark
leaks out?

It wasn't my fault I
scared my mother when I carried a
rat by the tail in one hand and
a mouse by the tail in the other
into our house
to find out what they were.
They *were* both dead.

Watching my very pregnant
mother move backwards at great speed
through the kitchen while
never taking her eyes off the
two questions dangling
by their tails
from my five-year-old fingers was
a most curious and interesting thing to see,
though I expected trouble.

When you look at questions
and open doors that leak dark,
you have to expect trouble.

I knew I was in trouble when those
boys dared me to jump off
the highest cement wall in our neighborhood,
but a dare is kind of like an
unopened box,
you don't know what's inside until you look,
so I jumped

and landed on both feet feeling
the impact run up the
length of my bones and rattle my brain.

I squatted to keep from falling, and
looked up to see—
silhouettes of four boys
jumping,
floating past the cement wall three
times their height, arms flailing,
each thud shaking the earth
as their bodies hit hard, all of us stung
by flying dirt.

Then I found words.
They kind of snuck up on me, you know,
they're right in plain sound and sometimes sight,
we use them all the time, but one day
I was looking up an "N" word in a card catalogue,
the old kind that held a certain quantity of cards in a drawer,
and I found "Nun" and "Nuclear War" in the same drawer—
I shut it quickly and looked around,
but no one else had noticed.

*Then* in one day I found out
the letters "C.S.C." mean

>College of Saint Catherine
>Criminal Sexual Conduct
>*and* Customer Service Center...

How very slippery.
And almost as dangerous as a nun and
a nuclear war rummaging around in the
same dark, closed, space—

Soon after I found a poet, or she found
me; we were on the same bus and how
we started to talk poetry three seats down
and across the isle from each
other on public transportation, I'll never know.
But when we got off at the same stop
and found out we lived on the same block only
four houses away from each other, it
didn't matter that she was
old enough to be my mother, or I
young enough to be her daughter, because
we both knew in our hearts that nun and nuclear
war should not be kept together in the same
dark, closed drawer; it was dangerous.

But neither of us was afraid of danger;
we both wrote poems.

Writing poetry is like taking
a dare, opening a door even though
dark will leak out, jumping
off a tall cement wall, by yourself,
to land in the dirt, or maybe not land at all.

And it's no use wondering why
so many people refuse to accept
what poets have to offer,
or to listen when teachers speak,
or to move when the music demands it,
because I've learned—
they are afraid of the dark.

But without the shadows, how can
we see the light?

## Choking

I swallowed
the apple whole.
Not because I wanted to miss
the crunch,
dribbles of juice,
or teeth-torn bits
of fruit, tongue-tossed,
slipping down my throat—

But deadlines demanded
denial.
Forget touch, taste, smell,
let the stomach preside, take over,
dissolve & digest
each sacred
separate
particle of apple;
send each bit
shooting through blood, tissue & bone
to nipples, fingertips, brain and mouth—

A mouth that opens
to swallow apples whole

chokes the heart on what isn't there.

# Rooted in White Space

*for Kim*

The seed will explode,
open,
become what it is meant to be.

Better
that you direct its growth,
extract and plant the seedling
where it can blossom.

It hurts less, you see,
to grow a poem
outside one's body.
Don't let it
devour your brain
eat your spirit
imagine—
rootlets reaching
through your eye sockets,
budding leaves straining for the sun.

Much better that it flows from
your fingertips,
falls into words,
black type on white paper,
naked,
exposed,
rooted in white space anyone can see,
read,
reap.

## Out of Context

*for Deborah*

Phillis Levin wrote,
"...part of me is missing; an essential portion..."

As if to say
she wasn't all there.
What missing part?
Her left hand had only four fingers?
Her right leg lost the knee joint
which connects thigh to calf?
What portion?
A peculiar opening
in the skin and muscle
which allows a casual passerby
to see clearly to the bone?

As a poet, of course,
all she says is suspect of deeper meaning,
layered parts packed into portions,
essential or otherwise.

Deborah disagrees.
She says,

"The point is stealing and writing fast."

part six:
Cancer

## Parts

Even when I'm not drawing
I am beginning to see
pieces,
individual parts,
kaleidoscopic shapes waiting
to spill into connections.

I never knew that would happen—
this fracturing, fresh vision
I couldn't control.

Then last night while
watching a wave
I saw what I thought
was a part—but it wasn't—
I wanted it to stop moving
so I could study it
and always
again recognize that
convoluted pattern tumbling inside the wave.

In microbiology
I looked inside blood to see
plasma, platelets, proteins,
fibrins—
looking for smaller and smaller parts
to figure out the whole.

The whole of my body
has no breasts now,
no ovaries, fallopian tubes, uterus,
all these parts
were cut off, or out of me,
and yet
I am still feminine, female...

Somehow
what is first seen
and understood
always
turns out to be more complicated—

like that identity
always moving within the wave.

# What Size?

When she asked me,
I immediately imagined myself
looking like Dolly Parton,
95% breast, 5% body,
and had a hard time not giggling.
It seemed so odd to be given a choice.

How many young girls
long for bigger, smaller, differently shaped
breasts that look like their mother's, older sister's, best friend's?

I've always considered our
society's focus on breasts
way out of proportion;
so it surprised me, when mine were no longer hanging around,
that my perspective suddenly slipped out of skew.

Maybe there is as much breast envy
as penis envy and it all starts
with the gender spot left vacant?

But men don't have to envy women's breasts.
Look around. All they have to do is
wait a few years and exercise less;
those drooping pecs will take care of the rest.

A woman, on the other hand, couldn't grow
a penis if she wanted to. And it's only
occurred to this woman to want to, momentarily,
when peeing in the woods or waiting in line
for the lavatory during intermission.

Truly, the whole envy issue
is as odd as being asked what size breasts
I want and walking out the door, a few
minutes later, holding them in my hand,
neatly boxed.

# RECONSTRUCTION?

You either get saline
implants or the surgeon
cuts and alters other body parts and
pushes and pulls them into place as bumps
on your chest which are
covered with scars and don't
respond or look like breasts.

This isn't my definition of reconstruction.

You don't get back
beautiful swells of flesh
intimately connected to your body
or nipples that restrict in cold weather
and respond to your husband's touch—
or even glands that overflow
with milk when your infant cries.

You get foreign lumps
with numb spots where the
nerves couldn't regenerate.

I don't have breasts anymore and sometimes,
that makes me sad.
But for those of you who keep asking,
no, I will never have breasts again.

There is no such thing as reconstruction.

## What is the word i'm looking for?

Castrate
Geld
Neuter
Spay

A feminine version of emasculate?
Femisculate? Or,
once those parts are removed,
is a woman just barren,
described as a state of being
no longer connected to an active verb?

Perhaps

I need not worry
about losing
my soprano range,
as I keep on singing?

## Mirror Image

Instead of breasts, two gently curved
scars span my chest
looking like lash-less eyelids,
closed in sleep.

My belly button, life-friendly
umbilical scar that it is,
wiggles incessantly, like a puckered,
inverted nose.

In exchange for my womb,
one rounded scar on my lower abdomen
trembles like a timid
smile about to break open.

I stare, then say to my husband,
"My naked body looks like a
sleepy happy face."

He walks up behind me, squints and murmurs,
"Hmm, I see...
a happy face with a goatee."

## Prostheses

It wasn't until
the sales clerk left the room
that I placed the flesh-like
shapes into the special compartments
and slipped my arms into a bra
for the first time in three years.

It wasn't fair
that once I hooked those hooks
my body thought my breasts were back—
remembered and rejoiced
in that gentle forward weight
which realigns stance and the way a woman
takes a deep breath.

Three years of scars and T-shirts didn't matter.
My body remembered,
would continue to remember,
all I had tried to reconcile or forget.

## Containers

No more breasts
holding milk
or even

ovaries
for small eggs
or fist-sized

uterus
for babies
but still a

live body
to walk in
breathe deeply

sing loudly
of love, of
joy, and death.

## Silhouette

Trees seem so solid
and comfortable;
does it mean something, now,
that my body resembles one?

This solid trunk
covered with the scars of living,
in flesh rather than bark,
reveals a story;
variously textured surfaces
tell of rain, hail, sunshine, and persistence.

My seeds have dropped, taken
on a life of their own; more and more leaves
drift daily in the autumn breeze.

What does this oddly limbed,
double-rooted silhouette,
stark against the rising moon,
have left to do?

part seven:
People, Ghosts & Angels

# She Who Must Be Obeyed

*for Dorothy*

It wasn't often
she graced you with a smile,
though not because of the prickly side of her nature;
she either didn't have her glasses on
and couldn't see who you were,
or else her thoughts were elsewhere:
on the servers, on the altar
on the readers, on the sound system
on the music she would soon pull out of the organ
out of the air,
out of her heart.

Passionate liturgist, exceptional musician,
she took me by surprise when she said,
"The practice doesn't matter,
the counting, the phrasing,
all the thought that goes into the before;
when you walk up to the mic
just open your mouth,
and sing the meaning of the words."

Those words spilled off her tongue
and into my mind,
reconnecting synapses,
playing along nerve impulses,
running the length of muscle and bone just like her fingers and feet
have run the length of many-layered keyboards over uncounted years—
dancing with joy,
swimming through tears—
she's followed our voices even into the cracks
where she said she couldn't go.

She-who-must-be-obeyed spoke
and now I can't help it;
whether I write a poem, or story, or novel, or stand beside the altar at church,
it all comes out the same;
my heart opens,
all pretense burns to ash,
and I sing the meaning of the words.

Amen

## Honky Tonk Angels*

I suppose one of them
kept me from carnal knowledge
at nineteen,
taking the shape of that girdle
which so defeated my young friend.

And perhaps they hover around bars
and street corners
disguised as shadows,
unseen,
but able to nudge
a sliver of hope
into a wobbly mind.

I expect in life
they were the kind of people
who would walk a precipice rim
leaning over the edge,
*learning*,
as only one who has fallen can greet
the unfathomable depths.

Humanity is such a motley crew,
it stands to reason
spirits would be so too;
the ones who choose to guard our steps
and follow those who wander in the dark,
who feel at home in fear,
and can,
with a sudden rush of wings,
set a wicked spin to pins,
where more angelic spirits dance
obediently.

   **Honky Tonk Angel*, a phrase from a song sung by David Allen Coe

## Immaculate Conception

It must have been a miracle.

All three of the conceptions I was involved in
were fairly down to earth,
sweaty,
involved actions and hungers I don't believe anyone
would refer to as immaculate.

Yet the concept remains full of mystery.

Entering a woman's body only *after* she says *Yes*.
God-spirit gently ripening an egg,
skirting round the role of human male;
Mary's *yes* creating the paradox of virgin and mother.

Note that God asked Mary,
allegedly gave her a choice, a chance to say *No*.
Although how many of us,
when faced with a talking angel or God,
whether we understood the question or not,
would have the guts to say, *No?*

Despite this, the question of choice and responsibility still remains.

If each one of us were to look back on our individual lives
and remember the one or two significant times
we might have said *Yes* instead of *No*—

Would we have awakened the next day
to a world filled with a mystery as earthy as a virgin birth,
our new existence the paradox of flesh and spirit
joined
and made whole?

# Ronnie

Short brown curls
lightly laced with grey
top her body, a
drumbeat in motion,
taut, energized,
each limb moving in
counterpoint to thoughts
welling inside—
curbed by the constant motion, repetition, improvisation,
needed to finish each day.

She walks from
class to class
teaching rhythm, explaining notes, counting
time, demanding pitch.
The music she directs quickens, blurs,
as students' eyes lock on her hands,
their breathing a soft pulse beneath the body of the music.
She holds her breath;
her hands fly.

She scans the line of music until
her eyes are caught and held.
She waits,
waits for the crescendo, a
soaring, rising rush of song;
her hands rise, tremble, tense—

she strikes the drum!

A throbbing of the heart
in steady, aching beats.

# Living Bones

*Part I*

He held the patient's leg firmly in
his hands, immobilizing
the fracture so the doctor could work.
The tibia stuck
out several inches, wedged over
the top of their patient's ski boot;
it looked just like the chicken
bones he'd chop and boil
to make soup.

He would swing the cleaver and bones would splinter,
flying about his kitchen, sticking to walls.
But before that he would manipulate
the joints just so, knowing always where to slice,
severing skin and sinew with one stroke,
just as the doctor pushed and pulled on this boy's leg,
also knowing where to place the knife.

*Part II*

He dreamed the chicken bones
danced round him as he sat in lotus
position on the top shelf of his refrigerator,
fitting easily between the milk and peanut butter.
He found it hard to breathe
as the circle of bones closed in about him,
strips of raw red meat atop each bone like a bloody flame.
The door closed.
The light went out.

He awoke panicked,
heart pounding,
inhaling the smell of blood,
feeling the movement of bones beneath flesh he held,
remembering the undead in his refrigerator, circling closer,
as he held the ghost blade in his hand
ready to place the knife.

# The Last Word

*for my father*

He falls into a story, any story
and rests inside each word's meaning
as he can no longer rest in his own bed,
betrayed by a disease
invisible to the human eye.

Healing words cover his body
like a soothing emollient
muting tremors, easing pain,
shortening moonlit hours
to mere minutes.

Enchanted words pull him
where he no longer stands;
instead of a flower stiffened and browning with age,
he can move again,
turn his face to the sun,
sway to the wild energy of the wind.

Wily, seductive words
defeat
the flaming nerves and clenching muscles
which mortar his body,
joint by joint, tissue by tissue,
into a stationary, human wall.

Each story's
carefully written words
take him cleanly to another universe
where all things are possible—

>     squatting to comfort a child,
>     walking up stairs without a railing,
>     turning to his wife in the night...

## Lost & Found

A divorced man
living alone
was halfheartedly looking
for still life objects
to sort and draw
but he found instead—wedding rings—
put away many years ago to prevent their loss
during a canoe trip into the wilderness.

My husband and I couldn't find those rings anywhere
when we returned.

And now this man finds them twenty years later
in his basement,
resting in a small, cloth-covered box
nailed to a rafter, draped with aging cobwebs;

gently opening the box
he discovers
this time—only the rings were lost.

## Breathing

At morning dusk
I roll over onto my back
and take deep, long breaths,
trying to mark each day
and be grateful
that I am still able to do so.
Much depends on breathing.

Whenever I can,
I love to stand in the dark
and listen to my grandson breathe as he sleeps,
in and out—in and out.
I so want him to keep on breathing.
I want you to keep on breathing.
What you do after that is up to you.
But much depends on that, also.

*Soundings* is GEORGIA A. GREELEY's first collection of poetry. A Minnesota native, born and reared on the West side of the Mississippi, she married young into a Saint Paul family and has lived East of the river ever since. She earned her BA in English and Art from the College of Saint Catherine. Georgia has worked as a graphic designer, staff writer, editor, production manager, 911 Operator, Fire Alarm & Medical Dispatcher, and a Public Information Officer for the Saint Paul Public Library. Since earning her MFA in Writing from Hamline University in 2001, she has been working as a free lance artist, writer, and teacher. Her three children are adults; her husband is retired; their dog and cat are living an active geriatric life. Georgia's writing includes poetry and memoir in *Sidewalks*, *Poetry Motel*, *Dust & Fire*, *Ariston*, and *Soup From Stones*, and short fiction for children in *Visions*, *Venture*, and *Highlights for Children*. She was awarded a Minnesota State Arts Board 2001 Career Opportunity grant for Children's Literature.

Georgia illustrated *One Hundred Tales from Sudetenland*, published by the German-Bohemian Heritage Society of New Ulm (ed. and trans. Karen Hobbs, 1999). Her artist's books and prints have been exhibited locally and regionally; she completed a six-month Artist's Residency at Minnesota Center for Book Arts in 2005. Georgia is one of four letterpress artists for Laurel Poetry Collective.

## LAUREL POETRY COLLECTIVE

A gathering of twenty-three poets and graphic artists living in the Twin Cities area, the Laurel Poetry Collective is a collaboration dedicated to publishing beautiful and affordable books, chapbooks, and broadsides. Started in 2002, its four-year charter is to publish and celebrate, one by one, a book or chapbook by each of its twenty-one poet members. The Laurel members are: Lisa Ann Berg, Teresa Boyer, Annie Breitenbucher, Margot Fortunato Galt, Georgia A. Greeley, Ann Iverson, Mary L. Junge, Deborah Keenan, Joyce Kennedy, Ilze Kļaviņa Mueller, Yvette Nelson, Eileen O'Toole, Kathy Alma Peterson, Regula Russelle, Sylvia Ruud, Tom Ruud, Su Smallen, Susanna Styve, Suzanne Swanson, Nancy M. Walden, Lois Welshons, Pam Wynn, Nolan Zavoral.

For current information about the series—including broadsides, subscriptions, and single copy purchase—visit:

www.laurelpoetry.com

or write:

Laurel Poetry Collective
1168 Laurel Avenue
St. Paul, MN 55104